TAKING ON THE
LEGACY OF
CHRIST

VOLUME 2

RJ SCHUHMEIER

Published in the United States of America

Brilliant Books Literary
137 Forest Park Lane Thomasville
North Carolina 27360 USA

CONTENTS

WORD OF WISDOM

I n this book, we will discover some of the characteristics of Jesus through life stories and examples, like knowing how to deal with the health of the mind, the heart, and the attitude. We will be learning what these things are? What can these things do? And learning how to apply some of these things in our daily lives, and so on and so forth, just to name a few.

CHAPTER 1:
Mind

The mind is a powerful muscle; that strengthens, or weakens by the thought process you engage in. The purpose of the mind is to remember and protect what you put in it. The mind can remember patterns, how you feel when somebody has done something to you. It can remember the past and what happened as a child, all the way up to adulthood, the mind is so powerful it can change the future if you want to.

When you think about the mind, the mind produces feelings towards someone. It can trigger good or bad thoughts that produces negative or positive energy that can replay movies over and over again. You can bring back the day, the year, and the month that things happened.

It is so critical to transform your mind because it can help you process what you want to say; or what you think about. Your mind will bring up things you want to remember or bring up the things you do not want to remember under the surface.

"So it is very important" to put good thoughts in your mind, even though you had a trauma or bad memories in your life; it doesn't matter if good thoughts and bad thoughts are processed because all you need is one image that can either damage your mind forever or transform it to renew your mind.

Renewing of your mind takes a lot of changes in your old ways. It takes time; you cannot rush it. It even takes time to build the bad habits that keep you bound or stuck. The mind allows you to keep repeating things over and over again until it becomes a habit.

The mind can be damaged by the fuel you put in it; the way how you damage it is by not being truthful with yourself, not being honest with yourself or with other people, and not understanding that bad habits can keep you bond, angry, and bitter like the danger of a stroke.

What's a stroke? You may ask! A stroke is damage to the brain from interrupting the blood flow. What causes a stroke? You may ask! It includes loss of blood supply, how you lose blood supply is not taking care of your body, and not eating the right foods, which will cost a blood blockage in the brain.

A stroke is caused by a hemorrhage bleeding in the brain. People with high blood pressure are at an increased risk of stroke, high cholesterol, and diabetes. Those who also smoke and those people with heart rhythm disturbances, especially atrial fibrillation are also at risk of a stroke. Your mind can take you to another place you may never come back from.

For example, taking drugs can interfere with the way your neurons sends, receives, and process signals via neurotransmitters. Some drugs, such as marijuana and heroin, can activate neurons because their chemical structure mimics a natural neurotransmitter in the body. This allows the drugs to attach to nerves and activate neurons. Although these drugs mimic the brain's own chemicals, they don't activate neurons in the same way as a natural neurotransmitter, and they lead to abnormal messages being sent through the network.

Other drugs, such as amphetamine or cocaine, can cause the neurons to release abnormally large amounts of natural neurotransmitters or prevent the normal recycling of these brain chemicals by interfering with transporters. This, too, amplifies or disrupts the normal communication between neurons. The body functions together whether you like it or not.

So if the physical mind can be damaged by doing bad habits and eating the wrong food, imagine if you didn't take control of your thought process, you would slowly be destroyed by the enemy over time. "To take on the legacy of Christ," you have to master the thought process in your mind.

I'm going to share a story about how my sister Darla conquered a situation in her mind.

When I was a young girl, I lived in Portland, Oregon, with my dad. My parents had gotten a divorce when I was three and my two sisters, at the time, lived with my mom, and I lived with my dad. My dad worked several jobs day and night. He worked as a security guard at night. So most of the time, I had to do and learn things on my own because my dad was either sleeping or working. For some reason, my dad enrolled me in a Catholic school, and I had to take a city bus across town by myself. I went to that school only in first and second grade; I was already given so much responsibility. I grew up as a latchkey kid, which meant I had to lock and unlock the apartment with the key around my neck. My dad was always at work, so I would always leave and return to an empty home before and after school.

On one particular day, I had a big challenge coming my way. I remember one particular time I was hungry in the morning, and there was nothing in the refrigerator to make breakfast. So I asked my dad if he could go to the store to get some milk and cereal for breakfast. And instead of him getting out of bed, he gave me his ATM card. He then instructed me to get twenty dollars out of the ATM, walk into the grocery store buy milk, cereal, and come back. As a child, it felt like I walked 3 to 5 miles from my apartment to the ATM machine, but in reality, it was maybe three or four blocks. During that walk to the ATM machine, I was scared and nervous. My heart was racing as I wasn't afraid of somebody trying to take me, but more so if someone thought I wasn't supposed to be at the ATM machine by myself and take my dad's card away from me. All I knew was that I was by myself and was instructed to get money from the machine and walk into the store to get the milk and cereal. My mindset was determined to fulfill the instructions that I was given, or else I'd stay hungry. Even though so many things were happening in my surroundings, God always protected me, and I was able to get what I needed and get home safe.

When you have a mindset to win, sometimes you might not even know what you are doing to accomplish your dreams, goals, or ambitions, or you might not know what's happening in life. But God is preparing you to do something great, even though you might not see it, believe it, or hear it. My sister Darla used her mind in different ways. One of the ways she expresses herself is by creating shirts, shadow boxes, cups, and more. One of her slogans was either "Designed by a Purpose" or Purpose by the Design. Either way, for inspirational artwork, go to https://www.designzbypurpose.com/

CHAPTER 2:

Heart

The heart is a muscle; that beats and pumps blood all around the body. A normal heart rate for adults ranges from 60 to 100 beats per minute. For kids, a normal heart rate is 220 beats per minute. The purpose of the heart is to pump blood to the organs and tissues of your body that needs the oxygen and nutrients it carries.

"The heart can carry a lot of toxins" that can weaken your heart over time, just like heart disease. Heart disease is a cardiovascular disease; this is a general name for a wide variety of diseases, disorders, and conditions will affect the heart and blood vessels.

The heart is composed of muscle tissue that requires a steady supply of oxygen in order to pump blood effectively throughout the rest of the body. Heart diseases can damage the coronary arteries, which provide oxygen-rich blood to the heart muscle. Heart diseases can also impair the functioning or structure of the heart and blood vessels. Coronary artery disease causes most heart attacks; it is the most common form of heart disease.

The different types of heart disease include; Atherosclerosis, which is a buildup of cholesterol, calcium, and blood clotting material on the walls of the arteries. The material that builds up is called plaque.

Cardiac arrhythmia is an abnormal heart rhythm; Cardiomyopathy is a weakened and enlarged heart muscle. A congenital heart defect is a problem with the structure of the heart.

Your heart can infect your body, how you feel, and how you perform. The heart can carry hatred, love, hostility, grudges, and happiness. To have a healthy heart, you have to have a healthy life; you have to let go of the things that hurt you. For you to do that, you should take a ten minute walk, do some lifting, eat fruits and vegetables, stop drinking your calories way, have some nuts, take a deep breath, and think positively.

When you change what you put into your mind, you can change what you put into your heart. The heart will bring out the feelings, and the feelings will bring out the actions. The actions will bring out the feelings, and the feelings will bring out the attitude in a person.

"The heart is the hidden key to the darkest secrets in your life," most people don't know about your sins, hurt, pain, and bad habits. These things will bring out the emotions you have. The important thing for your heart is to detox all of the unhealthy toxins that will surely cause a heart attack, like unforgiveness in your heart, anger in your heart, animosity in your heart, bitterness in your heart, and the most dangerous of it all, is not changing your bad habits will cause your heart not to function correctly.

A heart attack; is a medical emergency. A heart attack usually occurs when a blood clot blocks blood flow to the heart and causes death without any blood flow. The blood tissue loses oxygen when a heart attack occurs, and the heart muscle has lost blood supply and begins to suffer injury. The amount of damage to the heart muscle depends on the size of the area supplied by the blocked artery and the time between injury and treatment. The heart muscle is damaged by the heart attack; the muscle can later heal by the formal scar tissue.

"So it takes time for the heart to heal," if the body had a heart attack, it doesn't mean your life is over! You will have to stop! Think and reset. To reset is to change the way you eat, get active, stop smoking, and control your cholesterol and your stress. Remember, your heart holds a lot of stuff in it anger, hurt, pain, dark secrets, and hatred. These things will cause you to have a heart attack, and these things can cause you to have spiritual and natural bankruptcy.

CHAPTER 3:
Attitude

When you think about the word attitude, what comes to mind? What do you think about? When I think about this word it is either positive or negative. The word attitude also corresponds with the mind and the heart. But also connects with your emotions. Your attitude will bring out the actions in a person. To take on the legacy of Christ! You have to master all three components: *the mind, the heart, and the attitude.* Attitude is the first thing people will see; how you act before people start judging you as a person; having a good or bad attitude can change the atmosphere by setting a positive or negative mood.

"Having a positive attitude" can lead you to favor and blessings! And having a negative attitude can lead you to destruction, and destruction will lead you to a bad path, which can cause you to make bad decisions. Your attitude will allow you to complain and feel that people owe you something because of the mistakes you've made.

Your attitude can change your outlook and how you look, perform, and execute throughout your life. Your attitude will determine if you sink or swim. Most likely, people will do things for you with a good attitude.

Your attitude; will help you to get far in life! Your attitude will help produce promotions, your attitude will help increase blessings from others, and it will help you get favor from God. These things can change your life forever. People think you have to do a lot for good things to happen. But, really, all it takes is to make a minor adjustment; to do that, though, you have to learn, how to change your mindset; to do that, you have to have a positive attitude, for you to have a positive attitude, you have to have a positive mindset. A mindset is what you think about on a daily basis. There are 12 things you should remember about attitude.

1. Your attitude will affect your mood.

2. It is our attitude that determines our life.

3. It is impossible to succeed without others.

4. Before you become a winner, you have to learn how to become one.

5. The higher you go, the better attitude you should have.

6. Your mind can only hold one thought at a time.

7. The importance of human beings is to feel needed and wanted.

8. Look for the best in new ideas.

9. Don't waste valuable time.

10. Don't talk about others unless it's good or you are learning from the mistakes they made.

11. Regulate and have a confident attitude.

12. Treat people like they are the most important in life.

These 12 attributes will help you grow, help you get better, practice theses 12 attributes, and you will be surprised how it resumes and renews your life. If you want your life to transform, your attitude has to change as well. You can't have a different outlook on life; if you are not willing to change the way you think, if you think poorly, you get poor results. Success comes from doing and having a positive attitude.

I am going to share another story; about a person that is dear to my heart; her name is Suzette.

The Lord sanctified me at a very early age. I was 21 years old, and I'm now 53, but during my personal walk, I had to learn how to have a good attitude in the midst of my trials and tribulations; it was easy in the beginning because I was a young woman in the C.O.G.I.C. Stayed around the older mother's, I would go to the hospitals with my pastor and would pray for the sick with him, and with the mother's, and I loved that life, but I also recall during my earlier years the Lord had spoken to me and said he was going to take me through the Job to the Joseph experience all I knew back then was after reading about Job, I didn't dare want to go through that life. So many years went by after being saved, and I started going to the hospitals praying for others. Life then took a worse turn for me; I went through many tests and trials just like Job then I started to experience the Joseph experience while I was still in the Job experience from boils all over my body, a spot on my lung, Gastroparesis from experiencing abandonment, homelessness, with a roof over my head except it wasn't my roof, from my own family, so my once humble attitude turned to have a worldly attitude, of anger even hate, But God! But God! I didn't want to live because I suffered so much pain, but then after many years of going through a schizophrenic phase in my life, what I mean by this is that I was doing the same thing over and over again because I was not humble, but when I made up in my mind to finally go through all of my test like a soldier. Things started to look differently; although I had these trials, I was learning how to suffer the way Jesus did although I could never walk in his shoes, I was tired of going in circles. It wasn't necessarily with the same people; it was, at times, with new people in my life, but yet I was still going through the same issues. I knew I had to change my mindset and glory to the Most High God. I did it with the strength of the Lord, and I didn't have that spot on my lung anymore. I may have issues in my body, but my mindset has changed; therefore, my attitude has changed. All I can say is, I can do all things through Christ that strengthens me!

CHAPTER 4:

Encouragement

When I think about the word encouragement, it doesn't matter if you or I did something wrong, or right, or made mistakes; as people of God, we are exposed to give each other hope, encouragement, confidence, and love every single day. This comes with the territory of being a leader.

Being a leader! It is when we know when to encourage, we live in a time people are judgmental, angry, uptight, and demanding. The more encouragement we give people, the easier people appreciate the compliments and are willing to try harder in life.

When people are encouraged, people are easily motivated by the encouragement you give them; when you think about the word encouragement, it helps motivate, it helps loosen up the tension in the atmosphere. The atmosphere you set will change the mood, helping set up the mood will change the mind, the heart, and attitude of a person.

Before you become a leader, you have to be a servant. A servant is someone who learns, watches, and studies a person. I remember what Jesus was saying in *Mark 10:42-45.*

And Jesus called them to him and said to them, "You know that those who are considered rulers of the Gentiles lord it over them, and their great ones exercise authority over them. But it shall not be so among you. But whoever would be great among you must be your servant, and whoever would be first among you must be slave of all. For even the Son of Man came not to be served but to serve, and to give his life as a ransom for many."

The amazing thing about this passage is " if you know you are a leader," you should serve like you are not the leader; Jesus came not to be served! But to serve; to serve means to help, encourage, and uplift; this will help loosen up the range when someone is serving you. This is called true leadership.

As people of God, sometimes you will have to encourage yourself. Sometimes on this journey, you will not always have motivation, love, help, and encouragement. This is why the Bible says Hebrews 12:1-3.

Therefore, since we are surrounded by so great a cloud of witnesses, let us also lay aside every weight and sin which clings so closely, and let us run with endurance the race that is set before us, looking to Jesus, the founder and perfecter of our faith, who for the joy that was set before him endured the cross, despising the shame, and is seated at the right hand of the throne of God. Consider him who endured from sinners such hostility against himself so that you may not grow weary or fainthearted.

To be a great encourager, you have to wait, you have to be patient, and you have to wait for the right time to proceed to encourage. People are hurting going through, and sometimes people want you to listen to their situation because sometimes just listening is the best healing of all. Being an encourager can be different things like saying something positive, giving somebody a hug, listening to someone remind them of their strengths, let them know they are somebody. These things will help you to be an encourager, just like Jesus.

CHAPTER 5:

Prayer

What is prayer? Prayer is thanking God, worshipping, and asking God what you want to happen. Prayer comes in many forms of request! It comes in like a flood; we ask God for help, or we express our feelings toward God's word. Prayer should be our number one arsenal of getting up in the morning.

"Prayer sets up the atmosphere" for your day. When you set up the atmosphere, you are inviting the presence of God, which covers you and your family. Prayer protects the foundation you set for that day. Prayer is a weapon used against the enemy.

God will put a barrier over the enemy; the enemy can only go as far as destroying your purpose when you set up a barrier of prayer. When you pray, prayer can do amazing things. You can ask for healing, you can ask for forgiveness, you can ask for protection, you can ask for change, and you can ask for what you want. In *Matthew 7:7-8*, it says

7. Ask, and it shall be given you; seek, and ye shall find; knock, and it shall be opened unto you: 8. for everyone that asketh receiveth.

Prayer is asking, and when you are waiting for the answer, you will have to continue to pray because, most of the time, your answer is in your faith. Faith is believing, and believing is faith. When you have faith in something, keep praying until your prayer has been answered.

Before your prayer becomes active, you have to do some work! Let's say; you believe in a house, but before you receive your house, you have to do some work. Most people think they have to do a lot of work before "God allows a door to be open" for a blessing. Like Jesus said have faith like a mustard seed. It doesn't mean you have to have big faith, but small faith can eventually produce big faith! So my advice for you today is start small and think big. So let's get started.

The first thing you want to do is research who is the best realtor in your area. Second, what city, state, or country do you want to live in? Third, how much money do you want to put down if you want to? Fourth, which bank do you want to get your loan from, if you want to get a loan? Fifth, do you want to buy a home or build a home? Sixth, is your credit good.

When you set up your foundation and how you want to execute your plan your prayer starts to become active. God starts opening up the doors; start preparing for your prayer to be answered. The more you do the work, the more your prayer will be answered.

In the meantime, the enemy hears your prayers. The enemy will set up roadblocks, hurdles, and traps for you. The enemy does not like when you pray because the enemy knows the power of prayer. He knows how effective it really is. Sometimes we get discouraged because we want our prayers to be answered right away. We want our prayers to be answered in a day or two, a week, a month, or a year from now. If we don't see the soil, sometimes we believe our prayer is not working, God is not answering, or God is mad at us, but God will answer your prayer in these three ways. No, wait, or not right now, but in reality, it takes time for God to work. He wants to build your character, your faith, and your foundation to prepare you for your next season. The enemy is very limited in what he can do when you pray.

The enemy knows what the power of prayer can do. He doesn't want you to understand or unlock your full potential of prayer because prayer can do a lot of damage in a lot of areas. He has no control over when, how, or where you pray. As a matter of fact, it alerts him when you pray.

"In this movie Shazam," the wizard is seeking for a champion to see anybody suitable him to see who can take over his powers. When he dies, before the wizard gives his power to someone, he wants to make sure the person's heart is pure. To see if that person can pass the test, but in the meantime, the seven deadly sins tempt the person and say, don't be his champion, be ours.

The enemy knows what kind of true power the wizard has, so the enemy tempts the person to take their power, which is the eye, instead of the true power, which is the wizard's staff.

I'm saying this to tell you this when the enemy knows he cannot stop you. He entices you with what he can offer you instead of taking what the Lord Jesus has to offer and everything.

CHAPTER 6:
Bible

The Bible is a book of instructions for learning what to do and not to do? The Bible is a collection of the text of scriptures. Varying parts of the Bible are considered to be a product of divine inspiration a record of the relationship between God and humans. In the Bible, you will learn about many things like angels, the body, change, division, encouragement, forgiveness, grace, habits, patience, Jesus Christ, and many more.

The Bible is a book of knowledge and wisdom of scriptures and stories of real-life situations, so we can learn how to apply it in our daily lives. The Bible was written; so we can learn many things in life, but it would not be easy. But if you follow the instructions laid out in God's word, you will have blessings and favor.

The Bible has a "protection plan" to know how to deal with the enemy. The Bible shows you how to protect yourself against the enemy by putting on the whole armor of God, the belt of truth, the breastplate of righteousness, the gospel of peace, the shield of faith, the helmet of salvation, and the sword of the spirit. The enemy has only images and illusions behind which he hides his true motives, destroys the images, and breaks the enemy.

The Bible shows us what God can do! When we speak in the atmosphere, he can do miracles, he can heal, and he can set us free. The Bible is a book of truth, a book of believing, and a book of having faith when you read it. In the Bible, the passages make you think before you react. The Bible's truth will set you free if you ever notice when you read any religious books they will have part of the Bible in there. Most religions talk about these 10 things:

1. The Story of the Garden of Eden

2. The Story of the Great Flood

3. The Book of Proverbs

4. The Ten Commandments

5. The Canaanites

6. Isaiah

7. Angels and Demons

8. Heaven and Hell

9. The Holy Trinity

10. Aspects of the Messiah

The Bible influence other religions to write their own Doctrine.

The Bible was written between about 1200 and 165 BC. The New Testament books were written by Christians in the first century AD. God used many people to write his book. He used Moses, John, Daniel, Peter, Paul, and Jonah, just to name a few.

The Bible was written in detail: each book has its own topic. There are 66 books altogether. Genesis deals with the creation, Exodus deals with the freeing of the Hebrews, and the book of Leviticus deals with the rituals, legal morals, practices, and beliefs. The Book of Numbers deals with the wilderness, the suffering, Promised Land, and their complaints with God. And the book of Deuteronomy deals with the concern with old age moral issues and many more.

In the Bible, it says, hide the word in my heart that you might not sin against God. The Bible has the Old Testament, which deals with the old ways of living the old tradition, and the New Testament deals with the new way of living with a new tradition.

In the Old Testament, it was hard to live by because if you made a mistake or did anything wrong, you would drop dead, or you might not get a second chance at life, and if you did get a second chance of life, you have to make a sacrifice to God to let him know that you are sorry. In the New Testament, Jesus said in Matthew Chapter 5:17 *think not that I am come to destroy the law or the prophets: I am not come to destroy, but to fulfill.* This means he came on this earth to forgive and give us a second chance at life and to show us mercy if we do anything wrong.

The difference between Christianity; and other religions is that religion says do, and God says it's done! Jesus came on earth to save the lost, heal the sick and teach the broken so remember, the Bible is not to condemn but to fulfill.

CHAPTER 7:

Faith

How do you say you are active in faith? Faith is believing and trusting in something.

Faith starts off small. You have to build up your faith, and how do you do that? Good question. Let's think of something small you wanted so bad you wish, dream, and pray to God for that specific thing to come to pass. It is your act of faith. Whatever you believe in your heart, you will make happen.

Pastor Todd calls that crazy faith; Crazy faith is something you do for God, but you don't know what God is going to do. You have to have faith like a mustard seed, something so small you have to have faith and trust in.

When you sit in a chair, you don't know if that chair is going to hold your weight or not. All you know is when you sit down in that chair, you have faith in that chair. It will hold your weight. Faith is something you cannot see, but you know it's real.

You do not see love, but you know love is real. You do not see God, but you know God is real, you do not see miracles, but you know miracles are real, you do not see healing, but you know healing is real, and so forth, but you see the reflection in people to show those things are real.

To show if something is real, you show the actions; to prove what you don't see comes to pass. I knew when I was a baby my parents loved me. I knew as a toddler my parents loved me. I knew as a child my parents loved me. I knew as a teenager my parents loved me, and lastly, I knew my parents loved me when I became an adult.

My parents show me how to build my faith, so whenever I needed God, all I had to do was activate my faith. Whatever you experience in life will determine if you believe and receive the act of faith. Even though my parents love me, it doesn't mean other parents love their children.

We are a product of our environment. Whatever you were taught as a child, that's what you put out the most. If you put out hatred, hatred comes out. If you put out kindness, kindness will come out. Whatever you bring out the most, that's what you believe.

To take on the legacy of Christ! You have to believe things can change, or you can believe things can get better. We all fall short of the glory of God. We all have faith in something that is positive or negative. That's why we have to renew our minds daily. You can do good one day and bad the next day. Working on yourself is a daily fare. Sometimes you have to trade off faith, sometimes, you might not have faith in yourself, but someone will have faith in you.

Just like the story of the paralyzed man in *Matthew 9:1-7*

¹And he entered into a ship, and passed over, and came into his own city. ²And, behold, they brought to him a man sick of the palsy, lying on a bed: and Jesus seeing their faith, said unto the sick of the palsy; Son, be of good cheer; thy sins be forgiven thee. ³ And, behold, certain of the scribes said within themselves, this man blasphemeth. ⁴And Jesus knowing their thoughts said, wherefore think ye evil in your hearts? ⁵For which is easier, to say, Thy sins be forgiven thee, or to say, Arise, and walk? ⁶ But that ye may know that the Son of man hath power on earth to forgive sins, (then saith he to the sick of the palsy,) Arise, take up thy bed, and go unto thine house. ⁷And he arose and departed to his house.

Sometimes you will not have faith in yourself, but others will. Sometimes you will stay content in your faith because you don't see the manifestation of what God is doing. In our lives sometimes we have lazy faith because we don't see or trust in something we cannot see.

P.S. I just want to thank Pastor Todd and the transformation church for a wonderful series about faith.

CHAPTER 8:

Respect/Honor/Authority

Before you have respect, you have to have honor. Honor comes from respecting someone you love, and when you love someone, you honor them. Honor comes from caring, listening, and respecting someone's opinion or authority.

When you have authority, you should care for the people you help. Respect is earned and not taught before you have these three attributes of Jesus. You have to be a servant. Being a servant is a great tool for what to say, what to do, and when to do it.

Having honor is the principle of kindness: the first step of becoming a leader is to make difficult decisions. Respect is earned not given you have to show you can feel safe with that person. You know it's okay for both of you guys to express who you are. And when you disagree, you should listen to each other and expressing yourself by waiting and being patient.

As a leader, you have the right to show people you can listen and respect others and serve others when you can show that you are ready to become a leader; a leader is someone who can take an authority role, without being controlling and not forcing people to do things.

Although when you take the authority role, you have to have these six characteristics: intelligence, honesty, creativity, confidence, drive, and courage.

The different types of leaders are a pastor, bosses, directors, teachers, and many more. These positions have the authority to have the intelligence to know how to deal with people with different types of personalities. The second thing as a leader, you have to be honest with the people you are working with, what you expect from them, and what they expect from you as a leader in authority.

Not all leaders take on this role the right way; some leaders haven't learned what it takes to become a leader. Some leaders are born or given to, because of who they are or who they know, into a role they don't understand.

Being in authority is called give and take. It's like you're teaching someone something. They are learning from what you teach them.

Having authority as a leader is letting people express their opinion. Let people have creativity when you put them in a position to do so. When you are a leader, you should have confidence in that person. Whatever task you give them, they are capable of doing.

As a boss, pastor, or leader, in general, you should have the drive, passion, the motivation to push people to their potential. The most important role of a leader is to develop people how to become pastors, employees, bosses, managers, and workers in the marketplace. Whatever revenue they take, people should be able to build their skills to do whatever they want to do.

Jesus had the charisma and the charm to choose and develop the 12 disciples. Let's check out *Matthew 10:1-8. [1] And when he had called unto him his twelve disciples, he gave them power against unclean spirits, to cast them out, and to heal all manner of sickness and all manner of disease. [2] Now, the names of the twelve apostles are these; the first, Simon, who is called Peter, and Andrew, his brother; James, the son of Zebedee, and John, his brother; [3] Philip and Bartholomew; Thomas, and Matthew the publican; James the son of Alphaeus, and Lebbaeus, whose surname was Thaddeus; ⁴ Simon the Canaanite, and Judas Iscariot, who also betrayed him. ⁵ These twelve Jesus sent forth, and commanded them, saying, Go not into the way of the Gentiles, and into any city of the Samaritans enter ye not: ⁶ But go rather to the lost sheep of the house of Israel. ⁷ And as ye go, preach, saying, the kingdom of heaven is at hand. ⁸ Heal the sick, cleanse the lepers, and raise the dead, cast out devils.*

When you have respect, honor, and authority, your duty is not for you. It's for serving others, loving, helping, and teaching people how to work together just like Jesus did.

CHAPTER 9:
Obedience

L et me ask you a question? Let's say; your parents, ask you to wash the dishes and take out the trash. What would your reaction be? Would you do it with the enjoyment of your heart, or would you do it with complaining and anger in your heart, or would you do it with a smile on your face? Obedience is listening, sacrificing, and following instructions.

What is obedience? Compliance with another's authority.

Being obedient is one of the hardest things to do because we all like to do our own thing. Following instructions is teaching the foundation of how to be a servant before we become a leader. In the Bible, it says,

"Do not merely listen to the word, and so deceive yourselves. ..."Jesus replied, 'Anyone who loves me will obey my teaching.'"..."The world and its desires pass away, but whoever does the will of God lives forever." 1 John 2:17.

In the word of God, you will learn many different things about listening and falling. Instructions and learning how to be obedient [1] Learn how to do right, *in Matthew 5:21-48* [2] Submit to authority [3] Love others [4] Be humble [5] Be wise with money [6] Reaping and sowing [7] Conflict management.

The Bible is filled with so much information you can retain wisdom and knowledge without putting things into practice. To receive miracles, blessings, and favor. You have to be obedient to God's word because good things will start to fall into place. Being disobedient to God's word will lead you to curses and destruction.

Being obedient is doing something you do not want to do, but obedience is better than sacrifice. Sometimes people think you are kissing up to someone when you follow the laws of the land. When you honor God's word, you will put people to shame by the actions you do, actions speaks louder than words.

There are seven things you should know about obedience:

1. Pay attention to what they have to say.

2. Discuss concerns or issues in private.

3. Learn how to obey authority.

4. Understand what is expected from you.

5. Make sure you complete your task on time.

6. Avoid talking back, and

7. Act like you expect them.

If you do these 7 things, God will place you where he wants you to be, or he will place you where you want to be. Even if no one thinks you deserve the position. God will always promote you with blessings and favor when you are obedient to God's word.

Obedience comes with sacrifices if you do something for others or whoever is in authority, you will get rewarded spiritually or naturally. God can bless you spiritually, and naturally human beings only can bless you.

In Deuteronomy 28:1-3, [1] If you fully obey the LORD, your God, and carefully follow all his commands I give you today, the LORD, your God, will set you high above all the nations on earth.[2] All these blessings will come upon you and accompany you if you obey the LORD your God: [3]You will be blessed in the city and blessed in the country.

CHAPTER 10:
Responsibility

There are two questions you have to think about to have responsibility. 1. How to be responsible? 2. What do you do to be responsible? It is taking care of your business, your situation, and your task each day. Being a leader is taking on many different approaches in life, being willing to take on different types of task, and being willing to take on anything that goes wrong.

Being a leader, sometimes, it is hard for you to be willing to take your time and put one foot at a time, you have to be patient with your task and your situation. Being responsible is making sure everything is in order. As a parent, when you have kids, you have to make sure you feed them, clothe them, bathe them, teach them, and let them know what you expect from them.

The more you teach someone something it becomes a routine, a pattern, and a memory. When your child gets up in age, they will start to remember the routine you taught them. For example, when they get out of bed, they make sure they put their clothes on. They make sure they eat. They make sure they wash their face and brush their teeth. Comb their hair.

These types of things are things you will learn growing up. These type of tasks makes you have more responsibility as a person, parent, and adult. Having a pattern will always be a repetition in your mind. Your mind will always repeat what was taught and what was remembered growing up. Most of us will do the things taught as a child all the way up to adulthood.

As adults, you practice these things, you learn how to think for yourself, you learn how to communicate, you learn how to express how you feel, and you learn how to comprehend what people are saying.

Before you become responsible, you have to put what you learn to practice. What you don't know as a child, you will learn by watching, hearing, and practicing. When you keep on living, you will experience new things in life you will be using these basic materials at school, work, in public places, and at home. As you continue to progress in life, you will learn new skills, a new set of patterns, and a new set of rules.

In Matthew 28:16-20, [16] *Then the eleven disciples went away into Galilee, into a mountain where Jesus had appointed them.* [17] *And when they saw him, they worshipped him: but some doubted.* [18] *And Jesus came and spake unto them, saying, all power is given unto me in heaven and in the earth.* [19] *Go ye therefore, and teach all nations, baptizing them in the name of the Father, and of the Son, and of the Holy Ghost:* [20] *Teaching them to observe all things whatsoever I have commanded you: and, lo, I am with you always, even unto the end of the world. Amen.*

Jesus was teaching his disciples responsibility. Whatever was taught, it was learned. Whatever you hear, whatever you see, or believe, that's how you will receive.

The more valuable you become, the more responsible you become. There are nine things you need to know about responsibility: Take responsibility of your thoughts, feelings, words, and actions; stop blaming yourself and others; stop complaining; refuse to take anything personally; make yourself happy; live in the present moment; use the power of intention; feel calm and confident, and look for the good in people.

CHAPTER 11:
Excellence

When I think about excellence, excellence expires others and encourages me. I think about doing my best all the time. Having excellence, you are showing the quality of being outstanding or extremely good in something you love to do.

Although you should remember these 4 things about excellence, it is a mindset. It's a choice. Excellence doesn't happen by chance. Excellence is not a destination. The minute you think you have achieved excellence is the minute you need the most.

Excellence is the art of loving something that intrigues you on a regular basis. What do you love doing? Do you love to play sports? Do you love to sing? Do you like to play instruments? Do you like to write books? Or do you love to draw?

These things will empower you to think about what you are doing in life, whatever you put in your mind, to do you put the most effort in.

I remember when I was learning how to play the drums, I wondered how people played the drums. I always wonder how people remember what beat to play, how people build up their stamina to keep playing, and lastly, would I be any good?

I would practice the drums even though I didn't know what I was doing at the time. I wanted to learn so bad I used to practice by myself, and teach myself how to play, even though I didn't know what I was doing at that time. As a drummer, I didn't understand the mechanics of the drums when I was starting out. But that didn't stop me! I wanted to be the best, so I practiced, watched, played, and I put all my time and effort into teaching myself how to play. Even though it took many years and months of work and it wasn't easy, but I stuck with it, and now I am one of the best drummers ever lived.

In the meantime, I had to learn what was the best way to learn how to play the drums and because I have cerebral palsy, I had to work a lot harder than anybody else, so I had to figure out what was the best way for me to play.

So when you think about excellence, you have to practice on a daily basis to show yourself approval. When you put in the time to practice, you get better day by day. You might not see your improvement, but time and effort will tell.

CHAPTER 12:

Chosen

Being chosen is something you never think about. It is special in a unique way. When someone has a special gift, no man can take it.

What is special about God? You ask! God is one of a kind. He has power, he has gifts, he can create, speak things into existence, and do miracles. God is so special. He has gifts for everyone to enjoy on this earth. God gives us special talents and gifts to use on this earth on a daily basis for his purpose and glory.

Let's check out Genesis Chapter One, The Creation, God's first appearance, to show us what he can do without any assistance or help in making nothing into something. Before we talk about God, let's talk about how cars were made.

Now you ask, how can someone make something out of nothing? If it wasn't ever seen before, or it hasn't existed before, it will be a good question, just like Karl Benz, who made the first car. Now cars are so advanced. Before someone makes a car, they have to keep 11 things in mind:

1. Drawing/rendering is the first step,

2. Packaging is the first modification,

3. Computer and clay modeling comes next, as 2D rendering becomes 3D reality,

4. Full modeling then takes place with the chosen design,

5. Interior sketches and modeling,

6. Colors, materials, etc., are now chosen,

7. Dashboard and driver control elements are chosen,

8. Testing and refinement of materials is next,

9. Final modeling now takes place as the interior and exterior combined,

10. Model approval is given,

11. Final engineering and production concept complete, and production begins.

Evolution says there was a Big Bang, some type of sphere of how the world was created, and how humans evolved from monkeys and we developed with different types of species. If we did evolve, we wouldn't have the understanding of human beings having creative ideas about what happened, how it happened, who was there, and who wasn't there.

I think if nothing was created and everything evolved, we shouldn't have any creative ideas about how everything was created on this earth. Scientist deals with the explanations of how everything was formed and made, and religion deals with institutions, traditions of practice, literature, texts, and stories.

"Everybody has the right to their own opinion"; however, you should have faith in what you believe in. Now let's get back to the topic of how the world was made in the Book of Genesis and how God created the heavens and the Earth.

[1] In the beginning God created the Heaven and Earth. [2] And the earth was without form, and void; and darkness was upon the face of the deep. And the Spirit of God moved upon the face of the waters. [3] And God said, Let there be light: and there was light. [4] And God saw the light, that it was good: and God divided the light from the darkness. [5] And God called the light Day, and the darkness he called Night. And the evening and the morning — the first day. [6] And God said, Let there be a firmament in the midst of the waters, and let it divide the waters from the waters. [7] And God made the firmament, and divided the waters which were under the firmament from the waters which were above the firmament: and it was so. [8] And God called the firmament "Heaven." And the evening and the morning — the second day. [9] And God said, "Let the waters under the heaven be gathered together unto one place, and let the dry land appear." And it was so. [10] And God called the dry land "Earth," and the gathering together of the waters called "Seas," and God saw that it was good. [11] And God said, let the earth bring forth grass, the herb yielding seed, and the fruit tree yielding fruit after his kind, whose seed is in itself, upon the earth: and it was so. [12] And the earth brought forth grass, and herb yielding seed after his kind, and the tree yielding fruit, whose seed was in itself, after his kind: and God saw that it was good. [13] And the evening and the morning — the third day. [14] And God said, let there be lights in the firmament of the heaven to divide the day from the night; and let them be for signs, and for seasons, and for days, and years: [15] And let them be for lights in the firmament of the heaven to give light upon the earth: and it was so. [16] And God made two great lights; the greater light to rule the day, and the lesser light to rule the night: he made the stars also. [17] And God set them in the firmament of the heaven to give light upon the earth, [18] And to rule over the day and over the night, and to divide the light from the darkness: and God saw that it was good. [19] And the evening and the morning — the fourth day.

[20] And God said, " Let the waters bring forth abundantly the moving creature that hath life, and fowl that may fly above the earth in the open firmament of heaven." [21] And God created great whales and every living creature that moveth, which the waters brought forth abundantly, after their kind, and every winged fowl after his kind: and God saw that it was good. [22] And God blessed them, saying, be fruitful, and multiply, and fill the waters in the seas, and let fowl multiply in the earth. [23] And the evening and the morning — the fifth day. [24] And God said, let the earth bring forth the living creature after his kind, cattle, and creeping thing, and beast of the earth after his kind: and it was so. [25] And God made the beast of the earth after his kind, and cattle after their kind, and everything that creepeth upon the earth after his kind: and God saw that it was good. [26] And God said, Let us make man in our image, after our likeness: and let them have dominion over the fish of the sea, and over the fowl of the air, and over the cattle, and over all the earth, and over every creeping thing that creepeth upon the earth. [27] So God created man in his own image, in the image of God he created them; male and female he created them. [28] And God blessed them, and God said unto them, be fruitful, and multiply, and replenish the earth.

God gives us talents and gifts to use to build our empire, to build opportunities for success in many more.

The special thing about the gifts God gives us; you can learn how to use your gift to help others, you can learn how to build your gift for more experience and finally you can learn how to use your gift to build technique.

When you are a part of God's children, there are rules and regulations you have to follow before God puts his hand on something. Before God gives a gift, he might give you a test like a job, or God will give you instructions on how to use your gift like Samson before blessing you with that special gift.

Let's check out the last story of Samson and Delilah in the book of Judges, how God can use a special someone to help, to set free, and deliver his people from the Philistines.

6 ¹ And the children of Israel did evil again in the sight of the LORD, and the LORD delivered them into the hand of the Philistines forty years. ² And there was a certain man of Zorah, of the family of the Danites, whose name was Manoah; and his wife was barren, and bare not. ³ And the angel of the LORD appeared unto the woman, and said unto her, Behold now, thou art barren, and bearest not: but thou shalt conceive, and bear a son. ⁴ Now therefore beware, I pray thee, and drink not wine nor strong drink, and eat not any unclean thing: ⁵ For, lo, thou shalt conceive, and bear a son; and no razor shall come on his head: for the child shall be a Nazarite unto God from the womb: and he shall begin to deliver Israel out of the hand of the Philistines. ⁶ Then the woman came and told her husband, saying, A man of God came unto me, and his countenance was like the countenance of an angel of God, very terrible: but I asked him not whence he was, neither told he me his name: ⁷ But he said unto me, Behold, thou shalt conceive, and bear a son; and now drink no wine nor strong drink, neither eat any unclean thing: for the child shall be a Nazarite to God from the womb to the day of his death. ⁸ Then Manoah intreated the LORD and said, O my Lord, let the man of God which thou didst send come again unto us, and teach us what we shall do unto the child that shall be born. ⁹ And God hearkened to the voice of Manoah; and the angel of God came again unto the woman as she sat in the field: but Manoah her husband was not with her. ¹⁰ And the woman made haste, and ran, and shewed her husband, and said unto him, Behold, the man hath appeared unto me, that came unto me the other day. ¹¹ And Manoah arose, and went after his wife, and came to the man, and said unto him, Art thou the man that spakest unto the woman? And he said, I am. ¹² And Manoah said, now let thy words come to pass. How shall we order the child, and how shall we do unto him? ¹³ And the angel of the LORD said unto Manoah, of all that I said unto the woman let her beware. ¹⁴ She may not eat of anything that cometh of the vine, neither let her drink wine or strong drink nor eat any unclean thing: all that I commanded her to let her observe. ¹⁵ And Manoah said unto the angel of the LORD, I pray thee, let us detain thee, until we shall have made ready a kid for thee. ¹⁶ And the angel of the LORD said unto Manoah, though thou detain me, I will not eat of thy bread: and if thou wilt offer a burnt offering, thou must offer it unto the LORD. For Manoah knew not that he was an angel of the LORD. ¹⁷ And Manoah said unto the angel of the LORD, What is thy name, that when thy sayings come to pass, we may do thee honour? ¹⁸ And the angel of the LORD said unto him, Why askest thou thus after my name, seeing it is secret? ¹⁹ So Manoah took a kid with a meat offering, and offered it upon a rock unto the LORD: and the angel did wondrously, and Manoah and his wife looked on. ²⁰ For it came to pass when the flame went up toward heaven from off the altar that the angel of the LORD ascended in the flame of the altar. And Manoah and his wife looked at it and fell on their faces to the ground. ²¹ But the angel of the LORD did no more appear to Manoah and to his wife. Then Manoah knew that he was an angel of the LORD. ²² And Manoah said unto his wife, we shall surely die, because we have seen God.

> *But his wife said unto him, If the LORD were pleased to kill us, he would not have received a burnt offering and a meat offering at our hands, neither would he have shewed us all these things, nor would as at this time have told us such things as these. 24. And the woman bare a son, and called his name Samson: and the child grew, and the LORD blessed him. 25. And the Spirit of the LORD began to move him at times in the camp of Dan between Zorah and Eshtaol.*

The Bible says many are called, but few are chosen. What does that mean, you say? Everybody is called to do the will of God, but few people will do the work of God.

FOCUS/ENTHUSIASM

Focus is paying attention to something you have to get done, or you want to get done, you have to have enthusiasm to even have the excitement or the eagerness to want to do something.

I remember watching Kobe Bryant on YouTube one day. He said to be the best basketball player you can be you have to practice, you have to train, how much you can, and how often you can.

If your job is to be the best basketball player you can be, you get up at 10 am and train at 12nn. You train from 12nn to 2pm you train for two hours, you let your body recover, eat, rest for a couple of hours, then get back at it at 6 to 8 then you go home, eat dinner, take a shower, then wake up again that is two sessions.

Let's imagine you wake up at 3am, train at 4am, 4 to 6, you come home, eat breakfast, relax for a couple hours then you're back at it from 9 to 11. You eat, relax, and recover, now you are back at it from 2 to 4, eat, relax then you are back at it from 7pm to 9pm. Look at how much more training you did by waking up at 3am. As the years go by, the separation between your competitors and your peers grows larger and larger.

You have to be dedicated and focused, just like Michael Jackson, with his music. Michael Jackson grew up with Fred Astaire, Gene Kelly, and Sherman. It all started when they had nothing to do they will sing together as family. It all started when the boys would ask their mother; what did you use to do when there wasn't nothing to do, she said she used to sing.

Michael Jackson started a vocal group when he was younger with his five brothers, Jermaine, Randy, Tito, Marlon, and Jackie. Their father, Joe Jackson, made sure they practiced again and again until they got it right. Their father believed his kids had to work twice as hard to become great.

Every Friday night, there was an amateur night at Roosevelt High School, where they would sing every Friday night. The Jackson 5 pretty much won every Friday night. The word got around about the Jackson 5. That's how they started their career, The Jackson 5.

Although when you become focused, you build enthusiasm. Enthusiasm comes from your talent. Your gift will show through your talent. Your talent is the skill you create over time.

To have a legacy, "you have to have the work ethic," just like Prince, when you think about Prince, you think about a musician, songwriter, and entertainer. Prince would write songs to escape his past. His past let him be damaged and compelled and look for a family in all the wrong places.

Prince would watch his father play at a club downtown in Minneapolis. Prince will never forget his dad was a jazz pianist. His dad had hard times. He would drink and smoke and tell others not to do so. He became a bitter man jealous of his son Prince.

Prince asked his dad to teach him how to play the piano. Prince would learn and struggle when learning how to play the piano. His dad would get jealous if he struggled or picked up the chords he taught him his dad told him the piano is a fine instrument.

His dad told his son you think you're better than me! Even though Prince was just learning how to play, his dad was so hard on him he refused to teach his son how to play," Prince will look at himself in the mirror and ask, "What is my purpose on this earth? As many of us would say"

He will ask himself what is right and what is wrong when he went to school, things were no better. He was the short black kid people laughed at him. When he was 16 years old, he wanted to be famous. His first love was basketball, not music.

Prince shot hoops hour after hour. What he realized he needed for basketball was height which he didn't have. When he was playing basketball, he was finding himself, but when he got older, he stopped growing. He realized that basketball wasn't for him he had to do something else.

So Prince turned to music and put all his heart and soul into music. Prince didn't let his shortness stop him from playing music, Prince would ride his bike down to the music store to get the new James Brown, and Prince played music excessively in a friend's basement.

Teaching himself how to play many instruments as he could, throwing himself into music with heart and soul. He didn't want to fail at it. He had the desire. He is going to win, he said to himself. If he doesn't make it, it's not going to be his fault.

People say black artists will not succeed in Minneapolis. That's why his father had a struggle to break through. After three years of mastering keyboard, drums, and guitar, the groundwork paid off as he appeared on the Mike Miley show.

He told Mike Miley that he taught himself how to play instruments, and he stuck with it he played music all the time, then, later on, people started hearing about him and talking about him, and he started to become known, he had a band, it was called Grass Central.

One of the mothers from Grass Central went to one of the recording artists named Mr. Moon. She told him there was a kid on the block who could play all the instruments. He said she wanted a demo tape of him playing, then Mr. Moon realized when he was listening to him play he knew Prince had talent, and that is how he started his career.

Sometimes as people, we have to go through hurt pain and struggle to focus on something to have the enthusiasm to want to do better in life.

There are three people I want to mention, and one of them is my brother DeAngelo, my brother DeAngelo wanted to be one of the best basketball players ever. He studied Kobe Bryant. He loves the game of basketball so much that he even coached at Monterey Trail High School to take his skills somewhere else.

Second is my sister Phoenisha, my sister Phoenisha was talented in track and field. She never practice track and field. She had natural raw talent. I think she started when she was in 11th grade but, not sure. What she did do was wake up early in the morning to start a routine of conditioning for the sport, and she got a full ride at UC Riverside.

Thirdly is my sister Darla. Every time before going to work, she gets up in the morning at 5am to exercise at the gym. Before going to work, she is so dedicated she wants to make sure her body is in the best shape possible.

To be a legend or to have a legacy, you have to put in the time, the work, and the practice to become great.

PS. The people I look up to who made a great impact are the following 1. Jesus Christ

2. Bruce Lee

3. Kobe Bryant

4. Michael Jackson

5. Prince

6. Whitney Houston

7. Tupac

8. Biggie Smalls

9. My parents

10. Michael Jordan

10. Bernie Mac

Who is yours?